Open, Stay

_____

A collaborative new musical

Book, music, and lyrics by Anna DeNoia
Orchestrations and arrangements by Joshua Villa

Uproar Theatrics

LICENSING & PRODUCTION INQUIRIES
Uproar Theatrics, LLC.
hello@uproartheatrics.com | www.UproarTheatrics.com

Open, Stay
Music & Lyrics By Anna DeNoia © 2022
Arranged and Orchestrated By Joshua Villa © 2022

Open, Stay is published by Uproar Theatrics, LLC
500 8th Ave FRNT 3, #1714 New York, NY 10018

ISBN: 978-1-968051-39-6
First Printing, January 2026

PRODUCTION NOTES

Transcribed here is *Open, Stay* as it was performed by the 2022 James Madison University Workshop cast. This iteration of *Open, Stay,* however, reflects only one of many many ways these songs and their characters could be connected. With the author's permission, *Open, Stay* may be produced:

1.) As a book musical with the script as follows

2.) As a song cycle with the music alone

OR

3.) Build-your-own musical! Each song in *Open, Stay* is a confrontation, confession, or realization— moments of shifting power, connection, arrival, or departure. Something always changes, something always happens in each song, but the " who" and "why" are left open. Creative teams are invited to invent their own characters, decide who these moments belong to, and build an original story inspired by the score— to create a custom libretto tailored to their cast and community.

The music and lyrics (with the exception of pronouns) may not be altered without the author's permission, though alternate keys are available upon request. While many productions have found the central image of a door to be effective, it is not required.

CAST OF CHARACTERS

CAST SIZE:
The musical as transcribed here has ten characters—
character names in the libretto refer to the title of the song
each character sings. Alternate keys for all songs are
available upon request, suiting any voice type. Roles can be
doubled for a smaller cast.
All characters' gender, age, and race are flexible.*

ARIZONA (The Arizona Song) is good at grand gestures
and terrible at goodbyes.

WHO (Who Do You Think You Are?) is certain they can do
no wrong. Still, they do wrong.

ANYWAY (Anyway, Anymore) is in love for the first time,
and BOY is it awkward.

PARANOID is a once, twice, three times scorned spouse,
driven to the brink by their partner's infidelity.

TIMING is a two-timing asshole.

STARS has been left behind and is aching for closure.

DEVIL (The Devil I Don't) is defeated, but not powerless.

HOW (How You Thought It Would Be) carries the heavy
weight of a broken expectation.

VOICE (I Thought I Heard a Voice) is grieving their spouse.

OPEN (Open, Stay) has been burned so many times before,
but still chooses love.

*See note on the role of PARANOID on page x.

SCENE 1: PROLOGUE

> *Onstage there is an open door. The full cast is
> positioned in a tableau around it. DEVIL and
> TIMING together. HOW and WHO together.
> HOW holds an umbrella. One by one, everyone
> exits through the open door as they sing the intro
> to FINALE.*

ALL

AHH
AHH
AHH
AHH

> *OPEN goes for the door last. It shuts on them
> before they get the chance to pass through.*

SCENE 2: THE ARIZONA SONG

> *Transition— Summer. ARIZONA enters, carrying luggage, weary from travel. ARIZONA considers the closed door.*

ARIZONA
PARIS FRANCE IS JUST ANOTHER PLACE
THE MONA LISA'S JUST ANOTHER FACE
THE PYRAMIDS OF GIZA ARE JUST ROCKS THAT
DO NOT MEAN
A SINGLE THING
WITHOUT YOU

THE PAINTED DESERT'S JUST A BUNCH OF SAND
AND I WOULDN'T CALL THAT CANYON GRAND
SUNSETS IN SEDONA AREN'T MEANT TO BE
WATCHED ALONE, YA KNOW
THEY'RE NOTHING, NOTHING WITHOUT YOU

> *ARIZONA nearly goes to knock on the door, then thinks better of it. Instead, they pull paper and pen from their bag and begin to write.*

CUZ YOU ARE
COLOR IN A WORLD OF GRAY AND
YOU ARE
LANGUAGE LOVE AND ART
AND YOU ARE
HISTORY AND MUSIC
MY WHOLE WORLD WITHOUT YOU FALLS
APART

> *ARIZONA's fantasy/memory. STARS enters. The two of them are together again.*

2

THE NORTHERN LIGHTS, THE SUN, THE MOON,
THE STARS
ONLY SHINE TO ME IF THEY ARE OURS
THERE IS NO PIANO THAT HAS EVER PLAYED A
TUNE
THAT WAS NOT A SONG FOR ME AND YOU

CUZ YOU ARE
COLOR IN A WORLD OF GRAY
AND YOU ARE
LANGUAGE LOVE AND ART
AND YOU ARE
HISTORY AND MUSIC
MY WHOLE WORLD WITHOUT YOU FALLS
APART

> *STARS exits. Once again alone in reality,*
> *ARIZONA approaches the door, letter in hand*

AND I KNOW
I'VE MADE NOTHING BUT MISTAKES AND
EMPTY PROMISES TO YOU
BUT I KNOW
THAT IF I SHOULD LOSE YOU
THAT WOULD BE THE WORST THING I COULD
DO

> *STARS, in reality and unbeknownst to*
> *ARIZONA, appears on the other side of the door,*
> *listening.*

I KNOW THAT I CHOSE TO GO AWAY
EVEN THOUGH I PROMISED THAT I'D STAY
BUT NOW I KNOW IT'S YOU ALONE WHO FILLS
THE OPEN ROAD
THE ONLY THING I WANT IS TO COME HOME

ARIZONA (CONT)

THE ONLY THING I WANT IS TO COME HOME
CUZ YOU ARE
YOU ARE
YOU ARE HISTORY AND MUSIC
AND THE ONLY THING I WANT IS TO COME
HOME

SO I PRAY YOU'LL OPEN UP YOUR HEART
TO SOMEONE WHO HAS LEARNED
CUZ THE MOMENT THAT I LEFT YOUR SIDE
I DREAMT OF MY RETURN
AND I UNDERSTAND IF THAT IS NOT A CHANCE
THAT I HAVE EARNED
BUT IF YOU WILL LISTEN I WILL OFFER YOU
THESE WORDS

> *ARIZONA takes the pen and paper and finishes writing the letter against the back of the door. It contains the following:*

MEET ME IN ARIZONA
WHERE I SAW YOU FOR THE FIRST TIME
I AM WAITING IN ARIZONA
I'LL KEEP WAITING
YOU CAN TAKE YOUR TIME

> *ARIZONA folds the note and slips it under the door. Still behind the closed door, STARS picks it up.*

MEET ME SOUTH OF SEDONA
WHERE I LOVED YOU FOR THE FIRST TIME
I HAVE LOVED YOU SINCE ARIZONA
AND I'LL LOVE YOU
YOU CAN TAKE YOUR TIME

4

YOU CAN TAKE YOUR TIME
YOU CAN TAKE YOUR TIME
YOU CAN TAKE YOUR TIME

> *ARIZONA exits. STARS opens the letter and reads.*

SCENE 3: WHO DO YOU THINK YOU ARE?

> *Summer. A cafe on a rainy day. ANYWAY waits
> tables. HOW checks the time and sips their drink
> across from an empty chair, nervously waiting
> for someone. There is an umbrella at their side.
> VOICE sits alone. OPEN enters through the
> door, startling ANYWAY.*

ANYWAY
(flustered)

Hi!

OPEN

Oh hey! I didn't know you worked here.

ANYWAY
(A nervous joke)

Oh yeah. I own the place, actually.

OPEN

Really? That's cool.

ANYWAY

Yeah! I mean. No! Um. I don't actually. Own it.

OPEN

Oh.

ANYWAY

I don't know why I said–

> *TIMING enters through the door and greets
> OPEN affectionately— the two have met up here
> for a date. TIMING pays ANYWAY no mind.*

TIMING

Hi.

OPEN

Hi.

ANYWAY

H/ello

TIMING

/Two please.

> *ANYWAY seats them. WHO enters, soaked from the rain, and sits with HOW. The following conversations overlap and move **quickly**. WHO and HOW are speaking to each other. TIMING and OPEN are speaking to each other. Italicized dialogue should be spoken in unison.*

HOW
Where have you been?

WHO
I'm sorry.

HOW
You're soaking wet.

TIMING
You look lovely

WHO
I ran through the rain to get here.

OPEN
Thank you

7

HOW
You ran through the rain? Why?

WHO
Because it was raining, and I needed to get here.
It's really kind of romantic, if you—

HOW
Pneumonia isn't romantic. Where's your umbrella?

WHO
I disagree. I'd happily catch pneumonia for you.

HOW
I don't want you to catch pneumonia. Where's your
umbrella?

WHO
You know what I mean. Like, if you needed me to—

HOW
In what world would I need you to— you do own an
umbrella, don't you?

TIMING
Do you have any siblings?

WHO	**OPEN**
Yes, I do.	*Yes, I do.*

ANYWAY
(to VOICE)
Will anyone else be joining you?

VOICE	**OPEN**
Just one.	*Just one.*
	A sister.
	She made me this necklace.

TIMING
Can I see?

(TIMING and OPEN lean into each other.
ANYWAY looks on with jealousy)

TIMING
It's beautiful.

HOW
I don't get it.

TIMING
One of a kind.

(ANYWAY moves to refill TIMING's water)

HOW
If yours is missing, why don't you just get another one?

WHO
Because it's not missing. I know where my umbrella is, I just–

HOW
So then why don't you–

(Distracted, ANYWAY spills water all over
TIMING)

TIMING
HEY!

ANYWAY
Oh my god, I'm so sorry.

*(TIMING, soaking wet, storms off to the
bathroom. ANYWAY frantically cleans up. OPEN
tries to help. WHO snickers at the commotion)*

HOW
Don't laugh at them.

WHO
What? It's funny.

HOW
It's rude.

WHO
Ok, what is up with you? Is this about last night? I told you,
I'm sorry that–

HOW
No, it's not. Not exactly.

WHO
You know you kinda made me nervous. "We need to talk".

HOW
Well–

WHO
No punctuation or anything.

HOW
Listen, I'm not sure how to–

WHO
How to what?

HOW
Look. You know I think you're incredible. I so admire how
passionate, and… generous you are. So know when I say it's
really not you, it's—

WHO
Woah woah woah. Wait. Ok *that's* funny.

HOW
What's funny?

WHO
You have the waiter make a big mess and then pretend to
break up with me? Is that the joke?

HOW
I'm not pretending to break up with you.

WHO
You're not? Then what are you…

HOW
(Heavy, silent beat)

WHO
No.

HOW
Like I said, it isn't—

WHO
Why? Because I wanted to stay over last night? We barely even fought about it.

HOW
I told, that isn't the—

WHO
I said I was sorry. I know I should have just left when you asked me, but I.... I texted you too. This morning, I texted you again that I was sorry and—

HOW
I know, I know, but—

WHO
This is so messed up. After everything I've done for you? After everything I've let you get away with, I make *one* mistake and—

HOW
Hold on. Get away with?

WHO
All I'm saying is if you wanna play games, stay in your own league.

HOW
WOAH.

WHO
And now after all the time, all the *money* that I have poured into–

HOW
Money?

WHO
Don't act like it's not true.

HOW
I never asked you to—

WHO
You didn't have to!

HOW
(sarcastic)
Well, that's very generous, very kind of you

WHO
It is! It is kind! I am kind, and *you* are… cynical! And ungrateful, and–

HOW
People are staring. Can you please just–

WHO
    I WOULD HAVE TAKEN THE FALL FOR YOU
    DOESN'T MATTER HOW FAR I WOULD HAVE
    FALLEN
    I WOULD HAVE GIVEN IT ALL FOR YOU
    ARE YOU TELLING ME THAT YOU HAVE
    FORGOTTEN
    ALL THE TIMES THAT I FORGAVE YOU
    ALL THE PROMISES I MADE YOU
    NOW I'M ASKING YOU FORGIVE ME
    AND YOU'D RATHER BE RID OF ME
    THAT'S A LITTLE HYPOCRITICAL

WHO (Cont)
> SO WE'LL CHALK IT ALL UP TO EXPERIENCE I
> GUESS
> NOT EVERYBODY GETS A SECOND CHANCE
> LIKE THE ONE I GAVE TO YOU
> FUNNY HOW I THOUGHT YOU'D GIVE ME ONE
> TOO
> NEVER THOUGHT I'D HAVE TO TAKE THIS
> BLOW
> I NEVER THOUGHT YOU'D BE THE ONE TO LET
> ME GO
> AFTER ALL I GAVE TO YOU
> SO I HAVE TO ASK YOU
> WHO YOU THINK YOU ARE
> WHO DO YOU THINK YOU ARE?
> WHO DO YOU THINK YOU'LL BE
> WITHOUT ME?

HOW
Stop it.

ANYWAY
(*holding the check*)
Hi! Um, I was just wondering if/ there was anything else we could—

WHO
Give me the check. I always take the check. /I *always–*

HOW
Don't do that
> (*WHO takes the check*)

I said don't–

After making a passive-aggressive show of pulling out their card, WHO hands the check off to ANYWAY

WHO
NOT LIKE I HAVEN'T APOLOGIZED
HOW MANY TIMES HAVE I TOLD YOU THAT I'M
SORRY?
AREN'T THOSE WORDS THAT YOU RECOGNIZE?
DO THEY JUST WORK FOR YOU, DEAR, AND NOT
FOR ME?
I'VE GIVEN NO EXCUSES
TOLD YOU ONLY WHAT THE TRUTH IS
TRUSTING THAT YOU'D UNDERSTAND
THE WAY I HAVE TIME AND AGAIN BUT
YOU'RE A LITTLE HYPOCRITICAL

ANYWAY returns the check, and WHO signs with similar passive-aggressive showmanship

SO WE'LL CHALK IT ALL UP TO EXPERIENCE I
GUESS
NOT EVERYBODY GETS A SECOND CHANCE
LIKE THE ONE I GAVE TO YOU
FUNNY HOW I THOUGHT YOU'D GIVE ME ONE
TOO
NEVER THOUGHT I'D HAVE TO TAKE THIS
BLOW
I NEVER THOUGHT YOU'D BE THE ONE TO LET
ME GO
AFTER ALL I GAVE TO YOU
SO I HAVE TO ASK YOU
WHO YOU THINK YOU ARE

WHO is on their feet now, making a scene. All eyes are on them. HOW is mortified

WHO (CONT)
WHO DO YOU THINK YOU ARE?
WHO DO YOU THINK YOU'LL BE?

HOW gets up, takes the umbrella, and walks out the door. WHO follows them out into the rain. The cafe disappears and the scene moves to HOW's front door.

I ALWAYS THOUGHT
I'D BE THE ONE TO MAKE THE CUT BUT
I WAS WRONG
YOU HAD IT IN YOU ALL ALONG
SO WHEN YOU WERE TELLING ME
HOW MUCH YOU NEEDED ME
WAS IT ALL A LIE?

WHO and HOW lock eyes for a moment before HOW shuts the door behind them. WHO is left alone in the rain with the closed door.

I GUESS THAT'S THE REASON WHY
WE CHALK IT ALL UP TO EXPERIENCE I GUESS
NOT EVERYBODY GETS A SECOND CHANCE
LIKE THE ONE I GAVE TO YOU
FUNNY HOW I THOUGHT YOU'D GIVE ME ONE
TOO
NEVER THOUGHT I'D HAVE TO TAKE THIS
BLOW
I NEVER THOUGHT YOU'D BE THE ONE TO LET
ME GO

AFTER ALL I GAVE TO YOU
I GUESS I NEVER KNEW
WHO THE HELL YOU ARE
WHO DO YOU THINK YOU ARE?
WHO AM I GONNA BE
WHEN IT'S JUST ME?

SCENE 4: ANYWAY, ANYMORE

ANYWAY stands at OPEN's front door, which is closed. They hold index cards, flowers, a box of chocolate, and maybe some other ridiculous, romantic paraphernalia. A teddy bear? Balloons? Whatever it is, it's overkill. They hype themselves up before finally knocking on the door. OPEN answers. ANWAY sings, reading from the index cards.

ANYWAY
I LIKE YOUR EYES
I LIKE YOUR SMOOTH COMPLEXION
NOW IN YOUR EYES
I SEE YOUR CONFUSED EXPRESSION
PLEASE FORGIVE ME, I HAVE NEVER DONE THIS
THING BEFORE
I JUST COULDN'T KEEP IT IN ANYMORE

OPEN watches ANYWAY struggle with the cards due to all the things they're trying to carry. It's somewhere between adorable and pitiful. They offer help.

OPEN
Do you want me to–?

ANYWAY
Oh, um, sure!

OPEN takes the flowers from the pile of things in ANYWAY's arms. ANYWAY continues reading from the cards.

I THINK YOU'RE SMART
YOU'RE COOL, CALM, AND COLLECTED

AND SO MY HEART
IS HUMBLY PRESENTED
AND I KNOW IT'S WEIRD THAT I JUST SHOWED
UP AT YOUR DOOR
I JUST COULDN'T KEEP IT IN ANYMORE

*In fumbling for the next card, ANYWAY
sends them all flying. OPEN helps ANYWAY pick
them up. ANYWAY continues trying to read from
cards that are desperately out of order.*

I WILL CATCH YOU WHEN OTHERS HAVE
MISSED YOU
NOT IN A LITERAL WAY
OF COURSE I'M NOT TRYING TO CATCH YOU
THAT'S NOT WHAT I WANTED TO SAY
IS THIS GOING OKAY?

*OPEN doesn't answer. Instead, they check back
over their shoulder through the open door
behind them. Not discouraged yet, however,
ANYWAY takes a new approach.*

ANYWAY
I'M GONNA START AGAIN
CUZ I'D REALLY LOVE TO BE YOUR FRIEND
AND I DIDN'T PLAN THIS PART
SO I GUESS I'LL JUST SPEAK FROM THE HEART

I WOULD LIKE TO SPEND A DAY WITH YOU
I WOULD LIKE TO SPEND MORE THAN ONE DAY
WITH YOU
I WOULD LIKE TO SPEND ALL OF MY DAYS IN
YOUR COMPANY
IF YOU WANTED ME

TIMING appears in the door frame over OPEN's shoulder. ANYWAY shrinks

ANYWAY (CONT)

ANYWAY
THAT'S ALL I HAD TO SAY
FEEL FREE TO TAKE YOUR TIME

TIMING, not at all threatened, takes the chocolate from ANYWAY, considers it, then decides to keep it.

I'M SORRY TO DISTURB YOU WHEN THIS WAS
ALL IT WAS FOR
I JUST COULDN'T KEEP IT IN

TIMING takes the flowers from OPEN, shoves them back at ANYWAY, pulls OPEN back in through the door, and closes it, leaving ANYWAY alone on the other side.

ANYMORE
ANYMORE
ANYMORE

Just as ANYWAY is about to leave dejected, a glimmer of hope. OPEN re-enters through the door, stops them, takes back the flowers, smiles at ANYWAY, waves goodbye, then goes back inside.

SCENE 5: PARANOID (VOICEMAIL #1)

> *PARANOID's home. They struggle to get*
> *themselves ready one-handed (putting on shoes,*
> *pulling on a jacket, fixing makeup, etc) while*
> *being comically incapacitated by their phone,*
> *which remains in their other hand throughout.*

PARANOID

HI HON, I HOPE
YOU HAD A NICE TIME AT WORK TODAY
DID YOU HAVE A NICE TIME AT WORK TODAY?
IT'S IMPORTANT TO ME
NEXT THING, I WONDERED IF WHATEVER WENT
ON AT WORK TODAY
OR WHOEVER WAS THERE AT WORK WAS MORE
IMPORTANT THAN ME

CUZ THIS IS MY SEVENTH VOICEMAIL, NOT
THAT I'M REAL CONCERNED
JUST WONDERING WHY NONE OF MY THIRTEEN
TEXTS HAVE BEEN RETURNED
AND OF COURSE YOU KNOW I TRUST YOU TO
THE ENDS OF THE EARTH
BUT YOUR SECRETARY TORI, WELL NOW SHE'S
ANOTHER STORY
NOT THAT YOU WOULD EVER DO THAT
AND YOU KNOW ME SO YOU KNOW THAT

I'M NOT PARANOID
I JUST DON'T LOVE THE WAY SHE SAYS YOUR
NAME
I'M NOT PARANOID
JUST A LITTLE BIT SUSPICIOUS
NOT THAT SHE'S REAL COMPETITION
JUST I KNOW SHE'S ALL RELIGIOUS
AND YOUR MOM HATES THAT I'M JEWISH

PARANOID (CONT)
AND I KNOW I SOUND RIDICULOUS
BUT FAR LESSER SUSPICIONS HAVE CAUSED
HEARTACHE AND HARM
AND YOU SHOULD KNOW IF WE DON'T TALK
THROUGH THIS
AT YOUR NEXT WORKPLACE LUNCHEON
I MIGHT BREAK ONE OF HER TINY CHRISTIAN
ARMS

They exit through the door.

SCENE 6: TIMING

> *TRANSITION— Fall. TIMING's apartment.*
> *TIMING and DEVIL sit cuddled up together*
> *intimately. OPEN knocks on the door.*

DEVIL

Did you order food?

TIMING

No
> (*DEVIL moves to answer the door*)

No, don't get up, I'll get it

> *TIMING opens the door, sees OPEN,*
> *then quickly steps outside and shuts the*
> *door behind them, leaving DEVIL inside.*

OPEN

Hi.

TIMING

Oh. Hi! You!

> (*they sing to OPEN*)

SORRY
SORRY I NEVER CALLED
IT'S FUNNY
WELL NOT FUNNY, BUT I SWEAR THAT IT
WASN'T MY FAULT
CAN'T YOU SEE WE'RE BOTH THE VICTIM
HERE?
MAKE ME THE VILLAIN IF YOU NEED TO AND
I'LL MAKE YOU MINE
BUT WE'RE BOTH VICTIMS OF CIRCUMSTANCE

TIMING (CONT)
I SWEAR TO GOD I WOULDN'T LIE
NOT I, NOT TO YOU
THIS IS TRUE, IT WAS JUST TIMING

OPEN
You can save it. I'm just looking for my necklace.

TIMING
Your necklace? I'll go look for it!

OPEN
Well can't I just–

TIMING
Be right back!

> *TIMING steps back inside, shutting the door on OPEN, and quickly starts getting ready to leave.*

DEVIL
Who was that?

TIMING
The food I ordered.

DEVIL
But you said–

TIMING
I *just* told you I ordered food. But they messed up the order, so I'm just gonna go—

DEVIL

Hold on. Something's up. You've been avoiding me for weeks, and now–

TIMING

(they sing to DEVIL)

LATELY
LATELY I'VE THOUGHT OF YOU
BUT I'M SO BUSY
JUST SO BUSY THAT THERE WASN'T A THING I
COULD DO
AND I GUESS YOU'VE PROBABLY TEXTED ME
I WOULDN'T KNOW SINCE MY CONTACTS ARE
ON MY OLD PHONE
SO MAYBE WE BLAME TECHNOLOGY
AND TECHNOLOGY ALONE
NOT I, SEE IT'S TRUE
IT WASN'T YOU, IT WAS JUST TIMING

DEVIL

Okay, but you didn't used to–

TIMING

AND NOW WE CAN'T GO BACK TO WHAT IT WAS
NO WE CAN'T GO BACK AS MUCH AS I'D LIKE
TO BECAUSE
I'M NOT THE PERSON NOW YOU THOUGHT YOU
KNEW
TIME PASSED AND I GREW
AND YOU GREW
AND WE GREW
AIN'T IT FUNNY WHAT TIME CAN DO

DEVIL

Okay. I could eat. Let's go out.

TIMING

Actually, I'd like to take tonight for myself.

DEVIL

Wait–

TIMING

We've talked about this. Time apart is healthy. And you know I don't like it when you try to control me.

DEVIL

I'm sorry.

TIMING

It's okay. Just lock the door when you leave, alright?

> *TIMING exits back out the door, charm at 100, to where OPEN is waiting.*

TELL ME
TELL ME HOW HAVE YOU BEEN?
IT'S FUNNY
HOW TIMING HAS BROUGHT US TOGETHER
AGAIN

> *TIMING whisks OPEN away, and they exit together. Behind the door in TIMING's apartment, DEVIL finds OPEN's necklace.*

SCENE 7: STARS

> *Fall. STARS enters, reading the letter ARIZONA
> left.*

STARS
WE WERE OUT AT A PARTY
I WAS THE ONLY ONE YOU KNEW
YOU THOUGHT IT'D BE FUNNY
IF SOMEHOW WE GOT ONTO THE ROOF
I SHOULD HAVE STOPPED YOU BUT I
FOLLOWED BEHIND
I SAID OKAY AND UP WE CLIMBED

> *ARIZONA appears— a part of STARS' memory.
> The two come together*

AND THERE WERE STARS
THERE WERE STARS IN THE SKY
AND THEY MUST HAVE ALIGNED CUZ THAT
NIGHT
YOU TOOK ME IN YOUR ARMS
WITH MY HEAD ON YOUR CHEST
AND THE REST OF THE WORLD JUST FELT SO
FAR AWAY
AND THAT IS WHERE WE STAYED THE REST OF
THE NIGHT
AND THERE WERE STARS
THERE WERE STARS IN THE SKY

> *They separate and the closed door moves
> between them*

YOU WERE LIVING IN BROOKLYN
AND I WAS STILL STUCK IN SANTA FE
THE DISTANCE WAS AWFUL
STILL YOU WOULD CALL ME EVERYDAY

27

ARIZONA opens the door and pulls STARS through it.

STARS (Cont)
AND FROM A WORLD AWAY
YOU'D SAY YOU MISS MY EYES
YOU SAID LOOK UP
LOOK AT THE SKY

They dance together.

LOOK AT THE STARS
KNOW I'M SEEING THEM TOO
AND I'M THINKING OF YOU TONIGHT
EVEN THOUGH YOU'RE FAR
FAR AWAY FROM ME NOW
KNOW THAT THERE IS NO MOUNTAIN HIGH
ENOUGH
OR VALLEY LOW, AND THEN YOU'D GO
AND SING THAT STUPID SONG
AND THE STARS
THE STARS SANG ALONG

STARS passes back through the open door. ARIZONA closes it behind them and exits.

THEN BEGAN THE WAITING GAME
ALL A SUDDEN SOMETHING CHANGED

STARS turns back to see the door closed. They try to pull it open again but It doesn't budge.

SPENDING NIGHTS AWAKE TO WAIT
FOR YOUR CALL THAT NEVER CAME

STARS reconsiders the letter.

AND I DON'T WANT YOUR SORRY NOW
I DON'T WANNA HEAR OF HOW
IT'S A SHAME, IT'S A PAIN, PEOPLE CHANGE
AND PEOPLE DRIFT APART
FOR ALTHOUGH IT MAY BE TRUE
THE ONLY DRIFTER HERE WAS YOU
LEAVING ME, WONDERING WHY, NO GOODBYE
WITH A STOLEN NOT A BROKEN HEART

> *Now back in reality at ARIZONA's front door,*
> *STARS knocks. ARIZONA answers. STARS hands*
> *the letter back*

SO I DON'T WANT YOUR REASONS
I DON'T THINK I'D BELIEVE THEM ANYHOW
AND ANYWAY
SOON I'LL BE LEAVING
THERE'S JUST ONE THING THAT I NEED FROM
YOU NOW

GIVE ME BACK MY STARS
WHEN I LOOK TO THE SKY
ALL I SEE'S THE GOODBYE YOU FORGOT
AND IT'S HARD
WHEN THE DAY TURNS TO NIGHT
TELL ME HOW DO I HIDE FROM
A SKY THAT'S FULL OF STARS
I THOUGHT THAT THEY'D BE OURS
AS LONG AS THEY'D SHINE

THEY WERE OURS
THEY USED TO BE MINE
THEY USED TO BE MINE
THEY USED TO BE MINE

ARIZONA reaches for STARS to comfort them.
STARS pulls away.

STARS(CONT)
THEY USED TO BE MINE

I NEED THEM TO BE MINE AGAIN
MINE AGAIN, MINE
DON'T REMIND AGAIN
REMIND AGAIN, REMIND OF WHEN
WE WERE FRIENDS
WE WERE FRIENDS IN LOVE
OR AT LEAST I WAS

WE WERE OUT AT A PARTY
I WAS THE ONLY ONE YOU KNEW

SCENE 8: THE DEVIL I DON'T

DEVIL's apartment. Again, TIMING and DEVIL sit together, TIMING's arm around DEVIL. TIMING gets a text, brushes DEVIL off, and exits through the door. Alone, DEVIL considers the necklace.

DEVIL
I'VE GIVEN TOO MANY CHANCES
I'VE LET TOO MANY THINGS GO
THESE LIES, THESE GAMES, THESE DANCES
AREN'T FUN
BUT THEY'RE WHAT I KNOW

I KNOW YOU DON'T TREAT ME RIGHT
BUT AT LEAST YOU TREAT ME
YOU ARE NOT THE MAN I NEED
BUT AT LEAST SOMEBODY NEEDS ME

At OPEN's apartment, TIMING knocks at OPEN's door. The two embrace and exit inside

I'VE BEEN HURT AND DECEIVED
AND YET STILL I BELIEVE
THAT BEING WITH YOU IS BETTER THAN BEING
ALONE
I SHOULD LEAVE, I SHOULD GO
BUT THE DEVIL THAT I KNOW
WILL STILL LOVE ME BETTER THAN THE DEVIL
I DON'T
THE DEVIL I DON'T

YOU SAY
LIE DOWN AND ROLLOVER
YOU TELL ME

TO SIT AND STAY
AND I CAN'T SEEM TO REMEMBER
A TIME I DIDN'T OBEY

YOU DON'T TREAT ME RIGHT, I KNOW
BUT WHO ELSE WILL TREAT ME?
YOU ARE NOT THE MAN I NEED
BUT I NEED SOMEONE TO NEED ME

DEVIL knocks at OPEN's door. OPEN answers.
DEVIL gives the necklace back to OPEN, letting
OPEN know that TIMING is, well, two-timing
both of them.

I'VE BEEN HURT AND DECEIVED
AND YET STILL I BELIEVE
THAT BEING WITH YOU IS BETTER THAN BEING
ALONE
I SHOULD LEAVE, I SHOULD GO
BUT THE DEVIL THAT I KNOW
WILL STILL LOVE ME BETTER THAN THE DEVIL
I DON'T
THE DEVIL I DON'T

OPEN goes back inside their apartment
and closes the door. TIMING approaches. OPEN
shows TIMING the necklace. TIMING tries
to get the necklace away from OPEN. They fight.

IF I SHOULD LEAVE
WHERE WOULD I GO?
I AM WITH YOU
OR I'M ALONE

AND WHO'S TO SAY
THAT SOMEONE NEW
WOULD TREAT ME ANY BETTER THAN YOU
YOU'RE THE LESSER OF TWO EVILS AND I
CONFIDE
MUCH PREFER YOUR EVIL TO MY OWN MIND
SOME MIGHT FEEL PITY FOR MY MISERY
IT'S THE PRICE THAT I PAY FOR SOMEONE'S
COMPANY

> *OPEN gets away from TIMING, exiting
> out through the door. TIMING exits after them.*

AND BEING WITH YOU
BEING WITH YOU

I'VE BEEN HURT AND DECEIVED
AND YET STILL I BELIEVE
THAT BEING WITH YOU IS BETTER THAN BEING
ALONE
I SHOULD LEAVE, I SHOULD GO
BUT THE DEVIL THAT I KNOW
WILL STILL LOVE ME BETTER THAN THE DEVIL
I DON'T
THE DEVIL I DON'T
THE DEVIL I DON'T

> *Back at DEVIL's apartment, TIMING reenters
> through the door.*

WILL STILL LOVE ME BETTER THAN THE DEVIL
I DON'T

> *TIMING and DEVIL return to sitting together as
> they were before, TIMING's arm around DEVIL.*

SCENE 9: PARANOID REPRISE (VOICEMAIL #2) / I THOUGHT I HEARD A VOICE

TRANSITION — Winter. The cafe. It's raining again. VOICE sits alone. ANYWAY wipes tables. PARANOID barrels through the door, even higher strung than their first appearance. With one hand still glued to the phone, they aggressively gesture a coffee order to ANYWAY. PARANOID sings.

PARANOID

HI HON, IT'S ME
REMEMBER YOUR WIFE OF SEVEN YEARS?
YES IT'S TRUE, I'M YOUR WIFE OF SEVEN YEARS
THAT'S A STATEMENT OF FACT
NOW CONSIDERING
THAT I'VE BEEN YOUR WIFE FOR SEVEN YEARS
I JUST CAN'T QUITE RATIONALIZE YOU NOT CALLING ME BACK

SURE YOU'LL SAY YOU'RE WITH A CLIENT, OR A MEETING WENT LONG
IF THAT WERE TRUE THERE WOULDN'T BE A REPRISE OF THIS SONG
AND OF COURSE YOU KNOW I TRUST YOU TO THE ENDS OF THE EARTH
BUT IF WE'RE BEING HONEST
YES I DID DRIVE BY YOUR OFFICE
JUST TO CHECK OUT TORI'S PRIUS
I COULD KEY IT, BUT I PROMISE

ANYWAY returns with PARANOID's drink, right at the height of PARANOID's destructive fantasy. PARANOID snaps into a big fake smile and nods thank you, fishing for their wallet

I'M NOT PARANOID
I'M JUST CALLING TO MAKE SURE YOU'RE
OKAY
I'M NOT PARANOID

> *Shoving their card at ANYWAY*

ALTHOUGH REALLY WHO COULD BLAME ME
AFTER NOT FOR PROFIT AMY
WHO'D HAVE THOUGHT AT A FUNDRAISER
I'D BE TEMPTED BY MY TASER

> *They get their card back from ANYWAY. OPEN*
> *enters the cafe. ANYWAY, distracted*
> *by PARANOID, doesn't notice.*

BUT I KNOW THIS TIME IS DIFFERENT
THOUGH I CAN'T QUITE PUT MY FINGER ON
THE HOW OR THE WHY
SO YOU SHOULD KNOW YOU'D LOSE ALL MY
RESPECT
IF YOU CHEATED ON ME WITH SOMEONE WHO
CHOSE TO END THEIR FIRST NAME WITH AN "I"

> *PARANOID exits through the door. OPEN*
> *approaches ANYWAY.*

OPEN

Hi.

ANYWAY

Hi!

OPEN
I'd like to speak to the owner?

ANYWAY

Rambling, grabbing at napkins, looking anywhere but at

OPEN

Oh, um. She's not here right now? We're actually getting ready to close, but I could—

OPEN

I'm kidding. That was a joke. I wanted to talk to you, actually.

ANYWAY

Oh. Oh! Look, I am so embarrassed about the way I—

OPEN

It's okay. I thought it was–

ANYWAY

I had no idea you two were like, *together* together, and I just -

OPEN

We're not.

ANYWAY

You're not?

OPEN

Not anymore.

ANYWAY

So?

OPEN

So, you said you were closing soon? Does that mean you'd be free to…

ANYWAY

Oh. Oh! Um. I mean, I could ask the owner.

OPEN

But didn't you say the owner—

ANYWAY

Yes, I meant me, I meant— I was trying to do what you—
yes! I mean. Yes, I'm done, I'm free, I'm, yes! Just let me
finish closing up, okay?

OPEN

Okay.

> *ANYWAY, frazzled, drops the stack of
> napkins, just like they dropped their stack of
> cards earlier. OPEN once again helps pick them
> up, and the two touch. VOICE watches this new
> budding romance, and is reminded of
> someone else. From their seat, they sing*

VOICE

I THOUGHT I HEARD A VOICE
COMING DOWN THE STAIR
AT THE SOUND I TURNED AROUND
THERE WAS NOTHING THERE
STILL I SWEAR
THERE WAS A VOICE
AND IF THERE WERE
I WOULD SWEAR THE VOICE WAS HERS

> *ANYWAY lets VOICE know it's closing
> time. VOICE thanks them and gets up to go.
> The scene shifts from the cafe to VOICE's home.*

VOICE (CONT)
I THOUGHT I HEARD A VOICE
SOMEWHERE DOWN THE HALL
WENT TO SEE WHAT IT COULD BE
THERE WAS NOTHING THERE AT ALL
STILL I RECALL
THERE WAS A VOICE
I'M ALMOST SURE
THE VOICE WAS YOURS

> *HOW, visiting as a friendly neighbor, knocks on*
> *the door, once again holding the umbrella, as*
> *well as a bouquet of flowers. VOICE opens the*
> *door.*

I'M REALLY DOING BETTER
ALL IT TOOK WAS TIME
THOUGH I THANK YOU FOR THE FLOWERS
AND FOR KEEPING HER IN MIND
BUT REALLY I'M MUCH BETTER
BETTER THAN BEFORE
SO I THANK YOU, BUT I'LL ASK YOU
NOT TO ASK ME ANYMORE

> *VOICE takes the flowers and says goodbye to*
> *HOW, closing the door behind them.*

I THOUGHT I HEARD A VOICE
AND THOUGH IT CAN'T BE TRUE
AM I NAIVE IF I BELIEVE
THAT SOMEHOW IT WAS YOU?

*VOICE watches the other couples (STARS
and ARIZONA, DEVIL and TIMING, ANYWAY
and OPEN, WHO and HOW) move around and
past VOICE, while VOICE searches among them
for a face that isn't there.*

ARE YOU HERE?
CAN YOU HEAR ME?
ARE YOU REAL?
LOVE YOU MUST BE
CUZ IF YOU'VE REALLY DISAPPEARED
HOW CAN I STILL HEAR

*VOICE is alone again with the flowers and
the closed door.*

YOUR VOICE
YOUR VOICE
YOUR VOICE
YOUR VOICE

SCENE 10: HOW YOU THOUGHT IT WOULD BE

> *It's still raining. HOW's apartment. ANYWAY and OPEN are together elsewhere. The following conversations overlap. WHO and HOW are speaking to each other. ANYWAY and OPEN are speaking to each other. WHO knocks at HOW's door. HOW answers.*

WHO
Hi

HOW
Hi.

WHO
Hi. Um, I–

HOW
You can step inside. It's pouring.

WHO
That's alright. No pneumonia yet.

HOW
You still don't have an–

WHO
That's actually why I'm here.
You have it. My umbrella.
I thought I'd um. Come get it back. So.

> **ANYWAY**
> This feels right.

HOW
What do you mean?

                        ANYWAY
Me and you. These last few weeks together.
You make me feel a way no one else has ever felt before.
I'm sure of it. No one has. No one could.

HOW
       (*retrieves the umbrella*)
I'm sorry, but this isn't yours. It's mine.
I've had it for almost a year now.
I'm always carrying it. You've seen me–

WHO
I know. You walked home with it from my place.
The first night you stayed over?
I mean, I don't have a receipt or anything, but—

                        ANYWAY
Have you felt this way before?

                        OPEN
Yes. Yes I have.

                        ANYWAY
And what did you call it?

HOW
I remember now. I'm sorry.
You're right. Here.
       (*HOW gives the umbrella to WHO*)

                        ANYWAY
I love you.

WHO
Well anyway

> **ANYWAY**
> I love you.

WHO
I guess I should go

> **ANYWAY**
> I love you.

WHO
Thanks. For the umbrella.

> *WHO takes the umbrella and exits, closing the door behind them. OPEN, suddenly overwhelmed, gets up and leaves*

> **ANYWAY**
> Wait. Where are you going?

> *ANYWAY follows OPEN offstage. HOW is alone in their apartment*

HOW
RAIN IS FALLING, IT'S A CROWDED SKY

> *STARS and ARIZONA enter– a manifestation of HOW's memory of that first night with WHO. STARS stands in for a younger version of HOW, and ARIZONA for WHO. ARIZONA holds the umbrella, and the two rush playfully together through the rain to HOW's door.*

RAIN IS FALLING, AND I AM WALKING NEXT TO
YOU
WALKING NEXT TO YOU

> *HOW opens the door for STARS and ARIZONA,*
> *and the two come inside. ARIZONA takes*
> *STARS' jacket, and they sit closely together.*

RAIN IS FALLING SO WE GO INSIDE
RAIN IS FALLING, AND IN MY MIND IT'S JUST
LIKE IN THE MOVIES
HOW YOU THOUGHT IT WOULD BE

THE BED IS WARM AND THE ROOM IS CLEAN
YOUR BREATH IS WARM AND I AM LEANING IN
TO YOU
LEANING IN TO YOU

> *STARS and ARIZONA lean into each other,*
> *but freeze just before they touch*

YOU KISS ME HARDER THAN I THINK I'D LIKE
YOU KISS ME HARD AND I GUESS IT'S NICE BUT
IT'S NOT LIKE IN THE MOVIES
HOW YOU THOUGHT IT WOULD BE

> *ARIZONA dances with STARS, dipping and*
> *turning them, before returning to their close,*
> *frozen position.*

NOT LIKE IN THE MOVIES, HOW YOU THOUGHT
IT WOULD BE

> *HOW circles the frozen pair, singing directly*
> *to STARS*

THEY MADE YOU THINK IT WOULD BE
DIFFERENT
THEY MADE YOU THINK YOU WOULD BE
DIFFERENT WHEN IT WAS DONE
THEY MADE YOU THINK IT WOULD BE MAGIC
AM I THE ONLY ONE?

   STARS and ARIZONA exit opposite ways.

RAIN IS FALLING AS I STEP OUTSIDE
RAIN IS FALLING AS I SAY GOODBYE TO YOU
GOODBYE TO YOU

   WHO crosses the stage, carrying the umbrella,
   and exits.

MY FRIENDS ALL TELL ME I SHOULD GIVE IT
TIME
MY FRIENDS ALL TELL ME, BUT I'M NOT SURE
WHY
CUZ IT'S NOT LIKE IN THE MOVIES, HOW YOU
THOUGHT IT WOULD BE
NOT LIKE IN THE MOVIES
HOW YOU THOUGHT IT WOULD BE
HOW YOU THOUGHT IT WOULD BE
HOW YOU THOUGHT IT WOULD BE

SCENE 11: PARANOID/ANYWAY (VOICEMAIL #3)

TRANSITION— Spring. The rain has stopped.
PARANOID enters, as always, one hand glued to
the phone. They sing

PARANOID
HI HON, I MAY
HAVE LEFT YOU A COUPLE MESSAGES
THIRTEEN TEXTS AND A COUPLE MESSAGES
IN A SIMILAR VEIN
BUT YOU CAN IGNORE
THOSE TEXTS AND A COUPLE MESSAGES
PLEASE JUST LISTEN TO THIS VOICEMAIL AND
I'LL TRY TO EXPLAIN

SO I WENT INTO YOUR OFFICE SINCE YOU
WOULDN'T PICK UP
AND SITTING THERE WAS TORI AND THEN ALL A
SUDDEN

DEVIL comes through the door. The two
lock eyes. PARANOID lowers the phone for the
first time.

SHE LOOKED INTO MY EYES
SOMETHING THERE I RECOGNIZED
A CERTAIN WAY TO FEEL ALONE
I THOUGHT THAT NO ONE ELSE COULD KNOW

DEVIL
I WOULD LIKE TO SPEND A DAY WITH YOU

PARANOID
AND WE SAT AND TALKED FOR HOURS

DEVIL
I WOULD LIKE TO SPEND MORE THAN ONE DAY
WITH YOU

PARANOID
GOT IN HER PRIUS AND DROVE

DEVIL
I WOULD LIKE TO SPEND ALL OF MY DAYS
WITH YOU

PARANOID
ALL OF MY DAYS IN HER COMPANY
HON, SHE WANTED ME

DEVIL
MEET ME IN ARIZONA

PARANOID
ANYWAY
WE'RE HEADED WEST THIS SATURDAY

DEVIL
I NEED SOMEONE, YOU NEED SOMEONE TOO

PARANOID
MY BAGS ARE PACKED, THIS IS GOODBYE
AND THOUGH YOU HURT ME AND IGNORED ME
STILL I KNOW HOW IT CAN FEEL
TO FIND YOU'RE SUDDENLY ALONE
I'LL HAVE MY PHONE

SCENE 12: OPEN, STAY

OPEN's apartment. OPEN sits alone,
considering their last conversation
with ANYWAY

OPEN

WE'RE NOT THE FIRST, WE'RE NOT THE FIRST
LOVERS
WE'RE NOT THE FIRST TO PROMISE EACH
OTHER FOREVER
FOREVER, IT'S JUST WORDS
AND YOU'RE NOT MY FIRST, YOU'RE NOT MY
FIRST LOVER
YOU'RE NOT THE FIRST ONE TO DISCOVER
FOREVER
I NEVER USE THAT WORD

ANYWAY enters through the door holding
a book, greets OPEN affectionately and
sits comfortably against them to read

BUT WHEN YOU SAY IT TO ME
SUDDENLY I BELIEVE WHAT IT COULD MEAN
AND SUDDENLY I SEE
THAT WHAT I THOUGHT WAS TRUE
ISN'T TRUE OF YOU

ANYWAY continues to sit and read, time slowing
as OPEN takes them in. Little moments of touch
— hair, hands, shoulders

CUZ YOU TAKE
YOU TAKE THE WORDS FROM MY MOUTH
YOU MAKE, MAKE ME LOSE MY SENSES
YOU BREAK, YOU BREAK THE WALLS THAT I'VE
BUILT

YOU TAKE DOWN MY DEFENSES
SO HERE I AM DEAF AND BLIND
AND FINALLY WIDE OPEN
FOR THE FIRST TIME

> *OPEN, once again overwhelmed, exits*
> *through the door, leaving ANYWAY behind. The*
> *other couples appear (STARS and ARIZONA,*
> *WHO and HOW) and reach for each other.*
> *OPEN comes between and breaks through each*
> *pair. The pairs separate and exit.*

I'VE LOVED BEFORE AND LIVED TO REGRET IT
LEARNED LOVE COULD ONLY HURT IF YOU LET
IT
SO NEVER, DON'T EVER LET IT IN

> *DEVIL and PARANOID appear, and OPEN is*
> *unable to break through them the way they*
> *broke through the others. This pair exits*
> *together*

BUT THE WAY YOU HOLD AND TELL ME YOU
LOVE ME
HAS MADE ME THINK THAT MAYBE THERE
COULD BE A REASON
TO OPEN, TO BEGIN

> *VOICE crosses, locking eyes with OPEN*

CUZ I NEVER THOUGHT I'D BE
SAFE WHILE SOMEONE HOLDS A PART OF ME
BUT SUDDENLY I SEE
THAT WAS I THOUGHT WAS TRUE
ISN'T TRUE OF YOU

OPEN returns to the closed door,
which ANYWAY opens and pulls them through

CUZ YOU TAKE
YOU TAKE THE WORDS FROM MY MOUTH
YOU MAKE, MAKE ME LOSE MY SENSES
YOU BREAK, YOU BREAK THE WALLS THAT I'VE
BUILT
YOU TAKE DOWN MY DEFENSES
SO HERE I AM DEAF AND BLIND
AND FINALLY WIDE OPEN
FOR THE FIRST TIME

BUT IF I TELL YOU I LOVE YOU
DO I KNOW THAT YOU WILL STAY?
IF TO LOVE YOU IS TO TRUST YOU
THOSE ARE WORDS I COULDN'T SAY
AT LEAST NOT UNTIL TODAY

I LOVE YOU
I LOVE YOU
I LOVE YOU

STAY

SCENE 13: FINALE

OPEN and ANYWAY exit through the door together, leaving it open behind them. The cast enters as they sing their lyrics. They end by restoring their opening tableau around the open door, but now PARANOID and DEVIL are together, OPEN and ANYWAY are together, and WHO stands alone, holding the umbrella

ALL
AHH
AHH
AHH
AH

ARIZONA	PARANOID + DEVIL
MEET ME IN ARIZONA WHERE I SAW YOU FOR THE FIRST TIME I AM WAITING IN ARIZONA I'LL KEEP WAITING YOU CAN TAKE YOUR TIME	I NEED SOMEONE YOU NEED SOMEONE TOO I NEED SOMEONE YOU NEED SOMEONE TOO

ARIZONA
MEET ME
SOUTH
OF SEDONA
WHERE I
LOVED YOU
FOR THE
FIRST TIME
I HAVE
LOVED YOU
SINCE
ARIZONA
AND I'LL
LOVE
YOU CAN
TAKE
YOUR TIME

MEET ME IN
ARIZONA
WHERE I
SAW YOU
FOR THE
FIRST TIME

I AM
WAITING
IN ARIZONA
I'LL KEEP
WAITING
YOU CAN
TAKE YOUR
TIME

ANYWAY
ANYWAY,
I JUST
COULDN'T
KEEP IT IN
ANYMORE

WHO
WHO DO
YOU THINK
YOU ARE?
WHO AM I
GONNA BE?

TIMING
AND WE
GREW
AND WE
GREW

OPEN
WE'RE NOT
THE FIRST
WE'RE NOT
THE FIRST
LOVERS

STARS
THERE
WERE
STARS IN
THE SKY
AND THAT
NIGHT

HOW
HOW YOU
THOUGHT
IT WOULD
BE

VOICE
I THOUGHT
I HEARD A
VOICE
AND
THOUGHT
IT CAN'T BE
TRUE

STARS
THERE WERE
STARS IN
THE SKY
THAT NIGHT

ALL
YOU CAN TAKE YOUR TIME
YOU CAN TAKE YOUR TIME CUZ
YOU ARE
YOU ARE
YOU ARE

ARIZONA
HISTORY AND MUSIC
AND THE ONLY THING I WANT
IS TO COME HOME

STARS	**DEVIL+**
MEET ME IN	**PARANOID+VOICE**
ARIZONA WHERE I	AND THE STARS
SAW YOU FOR THE	THEY ALIGNED
FIRST TIME	
	DEVIL+
I AM WAITING IN	**PARANOID**
ARIZONA I'LL KEEP	I NEED SOMEONE
WAITING YOU CAN	YOU NEED
TAKE YOUR TIME	SOMEONE TOO

OPEN	**HOW**	**WHO**
WE'RE NOT	HOW YOU	WHO DO
THE FIRST	THOUGHT	YOU THINK
WE'RE NOT	IT WOULD	YOU ARE?
THE FIRST	BE	
LOVERS		

ALL
YOU CAN TAKE YOUR TIME
YOU CAN TAKE YOUR TIME
YOU CAN TAKE YOUR TIME

ARIZONA
YOU CAN TAKE YOUR TIME

The cast begins to move into the tableau

ALL
AHH
AHH
AHH
AHH

ARIZONA
YOU CAN TAKE YOUR TIME

The tableau is set. ARIZONA exits out through the open door. End of play.

PROPERTY LIST
- Luggage
- Paper and pen
- Book
- Coffee cups
- Napkins
- Umbrella
- Necklace
- Flowers
- Box of chocolate
- Cell phone

ON THE ROLE OF *PARANOID*:

It's important to note that jokes made in *"Voicemail #1"* are made at the expense of the close-minded mother— *NOT* at the expense of the character's Jewish identity. As the lyrics state, this is a Jewish character— that being said, one of the central goals of *Open, Stay* is to create a customizable production with completely flexible casting. If your creative team does not feel comfortable authentically representing this identity, then the musical lick at measure 35 should be cut and these lyrics should be substituted:

> *"Just I know she's all religious,* ***and you're mom's so goddamn pious"***

Or, if profanity is off the table:

> *"Just I know she's all religious,* ***and your mom's always so pious"***

SYNOPSIS

Open, Stay is a musical exploration of how we love and how we lose each other. Spanning musical genres, it traces ten encounters —beginnings, endings, the complicated spaces in between, and even moments that arrive long after a relationship ends. Each song is a confrontation, confession, or realization– a shift in power, a sudden connection, or a final goodbye. Full of laughter, loss, and lessons learned, *Open, Stay* captures the emotional extremes of the skeptical romantic. Paranoia, grief, joy, jealousy, awkward first encounters, and bitter partings braid together to create a work that feels both deeply personal and widely relatable— a collection of stories about how we reach for each other, what we expect, and what we ultimately owe to those we love.

While *Open, Stay* can be staged as a traditional book musical or performed as a stand-alone song cycle, it is at its most innovative within an open, collaborative framework—as a kind of 'build-your-own musical,' where creative teams use the score to generate an original story of their own. Within this collaborative model, productions are invited to reorder the songs, create original characters, and devise a new story inspired by the score. Because each song is written around a moment of transformation, the material provides a dramatic backbone without dictating who each song belongs to. This allows creative teams to tailor the piece to their cast and community, shaping a libretto that speaks directly to the people telling the story.

The flexibility of this structure means no two productions of *Open, Stay* need ever be the same. The music and lyrics themselves remain intact (though alternate keys are available upon request), but the storytelling framework is fluid. I conceived this "build-your-own musical" model as a way of expanding how we think about authorship and collaboration in new works. Rather than a single, fixed narrative, *Open, Stay* offers a foundation upon which performers, directors, and communities can build something original. It is both a show and a tool for theatre-makers, encouraging them to put their own experiences, aesthetics, and voices into the work.`

—Anna DeNoia

www.ingramcontent.com/pod-product-compliance
Lightning Source LLC
Chambersburg PA
CBHW021004150626
46549CB00012BA/1254